Beginners Basic Guide
to Stock Market Investment Boxed Set

This boxed set includes:

- **The Dividend Millionaire: Investing for Income and Winning in the Stock Market**

- **Passionate about Stock Investing: The Quick Guide to Investing in the Stock Market**

**Beginners Basic Guide
to Stock Market Investment Boxed Set**

As long as the earth continues, there will always be a time for planting and a time for harvest. There will always be cold and hot, summer and winter, day and night on earth.

A wise youth harvests in the summer,

but one who sleeps during harvest is a disgrace.

Beginners Basic Guide to Stock Market Investment Boxed Set

Beginners Basic Guide to Stock Market
Investment Boxed Set
By
Alex Uwajeh

Beginners Basic Guide to Stock Market Investment Boxed Set

Legal Disclaimers

All contents copyright © 2012 to and written by **Alex Uwajeh**. All rights reserved. No part of this document or accompanying files may be reproduced or transmitted in any form, electronic or otherwise, by any means without the prior written permission of the publisher.

This book is presented to you for informational purposes only and is not a substitution for any professional advice. The contents herein are based on the views and opinions of the author and all associated contributors.

While every effort has been made by the author and all associated contributors to present accurate and up to date information within this document, it is apparent technologies rapidly change. Therefore, the author and all associated contributors reserve the right to update the contents and information provided herein as these changes progress. The author and/or all associated contributors take no responsibility for any errors or omissions if such discrepancies exist within this document.

Beginners Basic Guide to Stock Market Investment Boxed Set

The author and all other contributors accept no responsibility for any consequential actions taken, whether monetary, legal, or otherwise, by any and all readers of the materials provided.

It is the readers sole responsibility to seek professional advice before taking any action on their part.

Readers results will vary based on their skill level and individual perception of the contents herein, and thus no guarantees, monetarily or otherwise, can be made accurately. Therefore, no guarantees are made.

**Beginners Basic Guide
to Stock Market Investment Boxed Set**

The Dividend Millionaire: Investing for Income and Winning in the Stock Market

Introduction

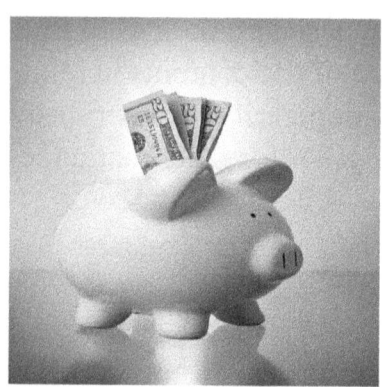

It's no secret that many people will retire without enough income to live on. Savings have dwindled to a point that simply won't sustain any type of realistic lifestyle once you stop working. If you're in this position yourself, how do you intend to pay for your expenses and lifestyle throughout your own retirement years?

More importantly, even if you're decades away from thoughts of retirement, how secure is your current income? The vast majority of people are highly dependent on the income they receive from their salary. When times are good, people don't often think about job security. They tend to spend almost everything they earn and save very little of the money they receive.

Yet, when times aren't so good is when people tend to start thinking about ways to supplement their income or even replace it altogether. This is when thoughts of investing often spring to mind.

Investing is supposed to be all about putting aside some of your own money into an investment vehicle designed to help increase the initial amount you put into it. This is where people buy into a particular investment and hope that their initial deposit grows enough to represent a profit. This is also known as investing for capital growth.

What most people don't realize is that it's very possible to also invest to create income. When you know where you should look, it's actually easy to invest wisely in specific investment vehicles that return a steady income to you, year after year.

Imagine if you had the ability to invest in something that could bring in a regular income for you as well as grow your wealth at the same time?

That's what we'll learn in this book. You'll learn about ways to develop a strong investment portfolio that is able to grow in value automatically – if you set it up the right way. You'll also learn exactly how to turn that portfolio into an income producing investment.

Are you ready to get started? Let's get into it...

Trading or Investing?

Before you jump into the concept of investing for income, it's important to understand the vital difference between trading and investing. Think for a moment about people who buy stocks at a low price and then immediately sell when the stock price rises enough to make them a profit. This tactic is called trading. Effectively, you're putting your money into the market and speculating that the price of the stock you bought might go up. It's a bit like gambling on the market moving in the right direction to create a profit based on your trade. The same concept is true for people who buy real estate with the plan of renovating it and then flipping it for a quick profit.

While there is nothing wrong with this form of wealth creation, it is essentially still trading.

By comparison, investing involved putting your money into a particular investment type and

Beginners Basic Guide to Stock Market Investment Boxed Set

planning to see a solid return over the long term. This might be buying an investment property in order to benefit from the rental income you receive over the years. It might be putting money into a high-interest bearing savings account and benefiting from the interest you earn.

It may also be buying into the stock market to earn dividends on the stocks you have sitting in your portfolio over the long term.

The real key behind becoming a Dividend Millionaire is to adopt a long-term investing approach. Even if the price of your stocks increases, your goal isn't to sell them and reap the profits. Your goal is to derive income from the dividends on a healthy, growing portfolio of good quality stocks.

In order to really develop a Dividend Millionaire mindset, it's important you take a long-term view to your investing strategies and tactics.

Beginners Basic Guide to Stock Market Investment Boxed Set

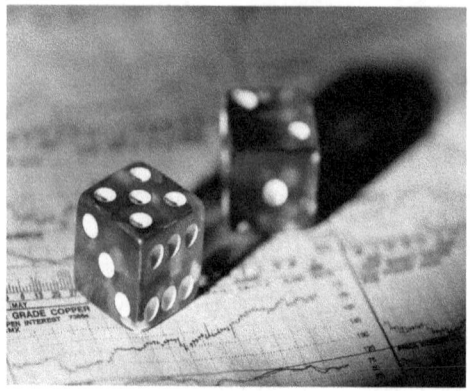

Understanding Dividends

Dividends are payments made to shareholders of a company from the profits made and income earned by that company. When a publicly listed company earns a profit it is able to distribute some of that profit between the shareholders. Some companies may choose to retain a portion of profits to put towards future company growth.

Even if you only own one share of an enormous corporation, you stand to earn dividends from it regularly. Dividend yields are most often allocated as a fixed amount per share owned, but they aren't always necessarily paid out in cash.

Forms of Dividend Payments

Cash Dividends – A cash dividend payment is actually the most common form of payment made. This is where shareholders receive a cheque for the amount due to them. In some cases, dividends may also be paid via electronic funds transfer directly into a bank account.

For example: if you own 100 shares and your dividend is quoted at $0.40 cents per share owned, you'll receive $40.

Scrip or Stock Dividends – Stock dividends are paid out in the form of additional stocks of that particular corporation. In most cases the stocks are issued as a proportion of any shares owned by the shareholder in that corporation.

For example: if you own 100 shares and your stock dividend is quoted at 5% reallocation, you'll receive 5 additional shares that will be added automatically to your stock portfolio.

Dividend Re-Investment – Some corporations offer a dividend re-investment option (DRIP). This is not quite the same as a Scrip or stock dividend. Instead, the issuing corporation may allow shareholders to use their dividend earnings to buy stocks to an equal value. There are also some corporations that may offer a small discount on the stock prices for choosing this option. As stocks are added to the shareholder's portfolio automatically, there are no commissions to pay.

Property Dividends – Property dividends can be paid out by a corporation in the form of assets. This might include stocks from the corporation in which shares are owned, or even a subsidiary corporation. However, these are quite rare.

Understanding Dividend Dates

When you buy stocks, you may notice that there will be an annotation next to it in your trading account. This will be either (ex-dividend) or (cum dividend).

Depending on when you buy or sell, these annotations can have the power to affect your trading strategy and your dividend earnings as well.

Ex-Dividend Dates

If you buy stocks that have been declared ex-dividend, they do not have the right to be paid the most recent dividend declared. However, if you sell your stocks during the ex-dividend date you still receive the most recent dividend payment due – not the new owner of those stocks.

Cum Dividend Dates

Any stock bought or sold 'cum dividend' has the right attached to it to be paid the most recently declared dividend payment.

Declaration Date

This is the date on which a corporation's Board of Directors will announce their intention to pay stockholders a dividend. The amount of dividend paid per share is usually confirmed and a payment date is also agreed on.

Starting Small for Big Gains

The biggest reason most people never begin investing is because they believe they don't have enough money to get started. This just isn't true. It's very possible to start with very small amounts of money and you certainly can begin investing in certain stocks in order to receive a dividend yield.

You see, it is very possible buy stocks with a relatively small amount of money. The key is to

Beginners Basic Guide
to Stock Market Investment Boxed Set

know which stocks to buy that will help you increase your stock portfolio more quickly. This might be by an increase in price, or capital growth, but it may also be because of good dividend yields reinvested back into your portfolio to help you build it even faster.

The key is to get started. Period. Even if you only have $100 to invest for now, that's enough to begin. In fact, you can even find brokerages out there that will let you start investing with just $25 per week. This doesn't sound like a lot of money, but it does have the potential to grow over time. You can always add to your stock portfolio as you start putting aside more money from your income each week to invest with.

We'll also go through some ways you can actively grow and increase your portfolio without using your own money in a later section of this book.

When most people start thinking about buying stocks on a relatively small budget, they immediately go looking for 'cheap' stocks. They seem to believe that buying 1,000 stocks at 0.10 cents per share will be better for them than buying 10 stocks at $10 per share for the same $100 investment.

Aside from this, those stocks selling at 0.10 per share might only give you a dividend yield of 2%, while the stocks selling for $10 per share might offer you a 7% dividend yield. The key here is to consider how much you'll earn back from your initial investment, along with evaluating the issuing company for strength and stability at the same time.

Never be persuaded to buy stocks simply because they appear cheap. If you're serious about building a strong dividend income, you need to focus on quality stocks from companies that consistently perform well and show positive earnings.

Cheap vs. Discounted

Of course, there is also a big difference between 'cheap' and discounted. The stock market is notoriously volatile. Stock prices go up and down regularly. If you tend to watch market movements, you can quickly become unnerved by how frequently prices seem to change.

This is where research will pay off in the long run for you. Cheap stocks can sometimes be an indicator of a poorly performing company. By comparison, discounted stocks may be a sign of a strong company suffering from price adjustments in a weak market.

Obviously, buying a good quality stock at a discounted price will give you far better quality stocks within your portfolio than a poor quality stock that you think seems cheap.

It's always better to look for quality stock to add to your portfolio rather than trying to shop in the bargain basement.

Cheap Stocks are Cheap for a Reason

When you see very cheap stocks selling at a few cents per share, think about how those prices may have been reached. Each individual stock is a portion of ownership of a much larger corporation. You may see extremely profitable corporations selling stocks for hundreds of dollars per share, but when you see corporations buying and selling stocks for pennies, there's something amiss.

There's also the fact that really cheap stocks often carry much greater risks. The company itself may not be in a position to post a profit, which means you won't be earning dividends from owning those stocks. The company might be struggling with financial issues or over-burdened with debts or faltering due to poor management. Each of these things has the capacity to cause stock prices to fall dramatically, which then makes them look cheap.

Choosing the Right Stocks for Your Portfolio

The stocks you should be focused on adding to your portfolio should include good quality stocks from strong, well-performing corporations. However, those stocks should also show a decent dividend yield at the same time.

Ideally, the yield you receive should be higher than the amount you could receive from leaving your money sitting in an interest-bearing bank account. However, always be a little wary of companies paying out extraordinarily high dividend yields.

Additionally, the price you pay for your stock should also be a consideration. Far too many investors have a belief that under-performing stocks should be a good buy opportunity. This happens when a company's share price is falling and many investors jump onto it, hoping that it may recover back up to its previous high price.

Unfortunately, there are corporations whose stock prices fall dramatically and never recover their previous high prices.

On the same note, there may also be corporations that are trading at lower-than-normal stock prices for short-term reasons. This could be an indication that the stock price may actually bounce back after that short-term under-performance.

This might seem confusing, but researching the company's trading history, profitability, debt and asset levels, and checking what previous dividend yields were like can give you a fair indication of which stocks will be better suited to your portfolio than others.

The most important thing to look at when you're evaluating any stock is to consider the future prospects of that company. Always assess each individual stock based on the merits of the company as a whole.

You should also research the recent dividend payment history of that particular corporation. This lets you determine whether a company has demonstrated a consistency in raising the amount of dividends they pay out every year. Companies such as these are dedicated to rewarding their long-term investors, so they're not likely to decrease their dividends in future.

Remember that companies that are performing well will only boost the amounts they pay in dividends if they're performing well. If any corporation you're researching seems to have stopped raising dividends, or actively reduced them, you should be slightly worried.

Dividend Yield Formula

Working out the dividend yield is quite easy. Take the dividend amount per share offered and divide it by the price you intend to pay.

Dividend Yield = Dividend divided by Price

As noted in the previous section, try to aim for strong, quality stocks with a good dividend yield.

Payout Ratio Formula

Another useful calculation to keep in mind is the payout ratio. The payout ratio is the amount of earnings paid out in dividends to shareholders from the issuing company. A low ratio indicates a secure dividend. This is because smaller dividends are easier for that company to pay out than larger dividend payments.

For example: if a company earns $2 per share and pays its shareholders $1 in dividends, the ratio becomes 50%. That particular company is paying out only half its income in dividends. Yet, it's retaining the other 50% to be reinvested back into the company for future growth.

The formula for calculating a payout ratio is as follows:

Payout ratio = dividends paid out per share divided by earnings per share

So, in this example, the dividends paid out are $1 and the earnings per share are $2.

$1 divided by $2 = 0.50 or 50%

A really high payout of over 75% is cause for concern, as that company is paying out dividends to shareholders and retaining almost nothing to pay for future company growth.

Diversify Your Portfolio

When you're researching which stocks to buy, always consider a variety of sectors in which to invest. You might do all your research and learn that mining companies or financial companies offer the best yields at reasonable prices for what you want to achieve.

But overloading your portfolio with stocks all in the same sector leaves you exposed to potential falls in your overall portfolio value if something happens to the companies within that sector.

Keep your portfolio safe by diversifying into a range of sectors. You'll find excellent companies within banking, retail, mining, IT and technology, commodities, and many others besides.

Ideally, your portfolio shouldn't contain any more than two stocks from within the same sector.

**Beginners Basic Guide
to Stock Market Investment Boxed Set**

Making Money When the Market Falls

Even very strong corporations can suffer falling stock prices during market crashes. During uncertain economic times, many investors feel the need to sell off their stocks in an effort to avoid losing money as the market falls.

Yet, smart investors understand that a strong, profitable, well-performing corporation may experience a temporary dip in prices that may well come right back once the market recovers. This is the ideal time to buy very strong stocks with decent dividend yields at a discounted price.

When you do your dividend yield calculations during these conditions, you should notice they appear a little better than normal. This is because the initial stock price is reduced, while the amount of dividend announced as being paid may not have been amended.

It's also worth mentioning that any stocks you already have within your portfolio may be suffering from falling prices, too. If you bought them at reasonable prices originally and your dividend yields are still strong, you may want to consider hanging onto them and riding out the market until it shows signs of recovery.

Know When It's Time to Sell

The objective of putting together a stock portfolio to earn income from dividends is to adopt a long-term "buy and hold" strategy. However, this doesn't always mean you need to hold stocks forever. There are times when selling good stocks makes sense. There are also times when it's wise to sell off any under-performing stocks.

While a falling market might represent some opportunities to buy great stocks at reduced prices, it can also be an indication to sell under-performing stocks within your portfolio. When a particular stock really isn't worth holding onto any longer, you need to know when to cut your losses and sell.

Remember, there should be absolutely no emotion in investing. This is about making an informed decision to benefit your portfolio and your overall dividend income.

Always monitor the performance of the stocks within your portfolio. Never be afraid to sell if a stock no longer offers you the performance you expect.

Should You Use Dollar Cost Averaging?

Dollar cost averaging is a particular investment strategy used by many professional investors. Unfortunately, it's not always the right strategy for dividend-yield investing.

Dollar cost averaging is all about investing the same amount of money regularly over a period of time into growing your portfolio. For example, say you commit to investing $100 per month every month for 12 months. When prices are low, you are able to buy more stocks with that same amount of money. However, when prices go up you end up buying fewer stocks with the same money.

For example, let's say you buy 100 shares of ABC stock for $60, another 100 shares at $65 and another 100 shares at $70. Your average cost for those shares will be $65.

For those people with only small amounts of money to invest, this can be an excellent way to gradually build up a portfolio over time. It allows you to work on setting up a regular savings plan and then put that money to good use over time as you can afford it. If you're buying a range of well-considered stocks throughout this time, you should find that you end up with a well-rounded, diversified portfolio of income-producing stocks.

Unfortunately, dollar cost averaging is all about buying exactly the same stocks every month, regardless of market conditions or prices.

For those with larger amounts to invest, dollar cost averaging over a period of time could potentially limit your investment. This is because only a small amount of money is being invested on a regular basis.

Statistics show that investors able to invest $1,200 up front are more likely to end up with a better rate of return overall in the following 12 month period as compared to those investors who choose to invest $100 per month over the same 12 month period.

Here's the formula:

Average Price Per Share = total cost of buying shares divided by number of shares

The whole point of doing this is to attempt to reduce the total average cost per share within your portfolio, which is intended to give you a lower total cost for those stocks you bought over that 12 month period. This lower total cost is intended to help limit your risk during market downturns.

It can also be helpful if you're trying to work out where to set your stop-loss order. If you know in this instance your average share price is $65, you might want to set your stop-loss order to 20% below this amount, which is $52. If your stock prices fall to this amount, it may be time to consider selling out and cutting your losses.

Always Use Stop Loss Orders

Within your brokerage account you should have access to placing stop-loss orders. No matter how safe or risk-free you think a particular stock might be, there will always be circumstances that can cause you to lose money.

Setting stop-loss orders are vital to any successful investing strategy. They allow you to:

* Protect against further losses
* Help to lock in gains

A stop-loss order is an automatic order that is triggered whenever a stock reaches a pre-determined price that you can set. For example, you might buy stocks that cost you $30 per share. After a week, the price may have gone up to $40 per share. You're able to set a stop-loss order for $35, so if the stock's price falls below this price they'll automatically be sold and you still keep your profit of $5 per share.

This is ideal for a short-term investor or an active trader, but it's not always the right approach for a long term investor. As your goal is to maintain a strong portfolio of stocks, you may want to set your stop-loss order to 20% or even 25% below the target price.

The reason for this is that the daily price fluctuations within the stock market shouldn't be your primary focus. It's only when really major pricing movements threaten your stock holdings that you should consider liquidating any long-term stocks you hold in your portfolio.

Types of Stop-Loss Orders

There are two primary types of stop-loss orders to remember: Market Orders and Limit Orders.

Limit Order

A Limit Order is when you set your sale price for your stocks to sell at a specific amount. For example, you may have purchased your stocks at $30 per share, but you could set your Limit Order to exactly $45 per share. It may take a while for the market to reach this limit, but when it does your order will go in. Unfortunately, there is a risk that Limit Orders may not be filled. This is especially true if the market is moving particularly quickly and the price shoots right past it on its way down.

Market Order

A Market Order is a little different in that your stocks will automatically be put on the market once the stocks reach the predetermined price you entered. So, if you've set your stop-loss Market Order to $45 and the market is still moving, you may not get exactly $45. Instead, you might get $44.90 or a price that is relatively close to where you set your stop-loss order.

Within your brokerage account you should notice the option to select the type of stop-loss order you want to place. You should stick to Market Orders when possible.

You also should remember that your stop-loss limits can be amended and updated at any time as well. This is excellent if your original stop-loss order was set at $45 but the market is still climbing at the stock price is now at $55 per share. You can reset your stop-loss order for $50 and know that you've protected your gains as the prices continue to rise.

Growing Your Stock Portfolio

The whole objective of this book is to show you how to create an income from dividends. However, in order to build your portfolio to a large enough size to produce a healthy income, you first need to grow it.

There are several ways to increase the size of your stock portfolio. You can:

* Invest more of your own money
* Wait for the stock prices to rise
* Re-invest your dividends

If you're serious about generating a realistic dividend income, you may want to work on all three of these options. Let's look at them all in some more detail.

Invest More of Your Own Money

If you're already on a tight budget and really don't have a large amount of money to invest, you can start out with a very small amount and still build up a strong portfolio easily. We mentioned this in a previous chapter, but it does bear repeating.

It's completely up to you how you manage your household budget, but if your goal is to earn money from dividends it's probably a wise idea to think about finding ways to cut your current expenses a little. When you can put aside enough money to buy more stocks, go ahead and place your trade order.

As mentioned previously, even $100 is enough to buy you 4 stocks at $25 per share. Of course, if you have more to invest then you'll find it a little easier to get started with larger amounts.

You also have the option of using a brokerage that allows you to invest as little as $25 per week to get started with your investing. This lets you put aside money on a regular basis that is then invested into growing your portfolio on a regular basis. Along with other portfolio-growth options, this has the potential to seriously grow your investment value to many times more than you paid for it over time.

Wait for Prices to Rise

This strategy is not always a good way to build any portfolio as stock prices can – and do – fall. Besides, putting all your hopes on the prospect of capital gains on stocks you've bought is a bit like gambling.

However, it's always a good idea to keep an eye on your overall portfolio value and individual stock prices.

Re-Invest Your Dividends

During the growth phase of building your stock portfolio, it's important to search for corporations that will allow you to re-invest your dividends. You want your dividends paid to you in the form of additional stocks added to your portfolio.

This approach means you will not be earning any cash payments from the dividends you earn at first. Instead, those dividend earnings will be buying you more stocks to add to your existing portfolio.

What's more, you're not paying any commissions or brokerage fees to have those additional stocks added to your holdings. This represents a saving to you, as buying those same stocks with your own money would have cost you those fees and charges.

Beginners Basic Guide to Stock Market Investment Boxed Set

As long as you're in the growth phase of your investing plan, always work on re-investing your dividends and receiving your payments in the form of more stock. As your stock holdings grow, the amount you earn from dividends will also grow. You may also find that the overall value of your stock portfolio increases as a result.

The longer you hold stocks within your portfolio, the more your returns are able to compound.

Imagine starting your portfolio owning only 20 shares of a strong, well-performing stock. After 10 years, your number of shares in that company could have grown to 2,200 shares – and that's without adding any of your own extra money. That's just the power of re-investing the dividends you earn and allowing the returns to compound.

When you add in the power of compounding growth, you suddenly have a strong portfolio that is increasing in value. At the same time, the number of stocks you own is increasing on its own, which further increases your dividend income. It's at this point you can choose to continue re-investing your dividends or switch it over to cash dividends and use it as your own income.

Leveraging for Growth

Once you have built up your stock portfolio a little, some brokerages will allow you to borrow money against your share ownership. This type of lending is called margin lending, and it's designed to let you borrow a certain percentage of the value of the stocks you own in order to buy even more stocks.

The idea of leveraging your existing portfolio isn't a new idea. However, it is one that should be used with caution. Borrowing money for the purpose of investing in the stock market can be fraught with danger. This is especially true if you leverage too highly or if you're not careful about how much you're borrowing.

Essentially, by borrowing some funds against the value of your existing shares, you have the opportunity to purchase even more.

The key to succeeding with this principle is to work out the calculations for how much your interest repayments will cost you on your margin loan and then work out how much extra you'll earn in dividend payments as a result.

For example: let's assume you have a portfolio with a value of $10,000. You may decide to

Beginners Basic Guide
to Stock Market Investment Boxed Set

borrow at a 40% loan to value ratio. This gives you an additional $4,000 to invest into the market.

Assuming you buy stocks that return 8% dividend yield, this gives you $320 per year in additional dividend income from just those new stocks you purchased. Of course, you also still have your initial $10,000 portfolio earning dividends as well. This is a total of $14,000 earning dividend income. Let's assume your total portfolio is returning 6% on average. This means you're earning around $840 a year in dividend income.

As your portfolio value grows, you have the ability to borrow even more money against it. This helps you boost your overall value, but it also raises how much you earn in dividends. As a result, if you stick to the dividend re-investment plan, you end up with far more stocks in your portfolio overall. And so it compounds again.

Unfortunately, margin loans are often charged at higher interest rates than home mortgages or personal loans. This is where it's important to work out exactly how much you'll repay on your margin loan. It's also vitally important to ensure you never borrow so much that your earnings don't quite cover the amount you need to repay.

Ideally, if you do borrow a small amount to increase your stock holdings, you should work out a way to repay your balance easily. This could mean using your own income to repay this amount, which also means keeping the balance within easily affordable levels. It could also mean strategically choosing one of your stocks to revert to cash dividends in order to use that cash to make repayments in advance as you receive it.

A Word of Warning about Margin Loans

Margin loans can seem like an easy way to increase your portfolio value and boost your dividend earnings at the same time. However, it's really important that you never leverage your borrowings too high.

The vast majority of brokerages will limit the amount you can borrow against your stock values to between 60% and 80%. This might be very tempting, but you'll be much safer to limit your borrowings to between 40% and 50% of the total value of your portfolio.

The reason for this is because stock prices do fluctuate. The market does rise and fall. If the market was to fall far enough that your stock values end up lower than your margin loan amount, you will officially go into "margin call".

A margin call is when your brokerage demands that you immediately reduce your outstanding loan amount down to an acceptable loan to value ratio. If you don't have the available cash to do this, your stocks will automatically be sold down in an effort to reduce your margin loan balance.

As margin calls most often happen during market downturns, this means the value of the stocks you're selling is also at a low point. You're getting less money for your stocks, the proceeds of which will then go to repaying your margin loan down to acceptable levels.

This situation can be more easily avoided by being very cautious about the amount borrowed. Always take the time to work through calculations as thoroughly as you can before attempting this strategy.

Going From Portfolio Growth to Dividend Income

During the growth phase of your portfolio, you really need to focus hard on dividend re-investment, plus adding additional funds from your own income whenever you can afford to do so. This will keep your level of stock holdings rising, which should result in an increased portfolio value.

However, the whole object of doing this is to create an income from the dividends you earn. This is where you need to have grown your portfolio to such a level that the income earned is substantial enough to supplement your income, or even replace it.

Just as you nominated to re-invest your dividends initially to grow your portfolio value, you can also nominate to return to cash dividend payments when it suits you. From this point, you're able to use that cash income how you choose.

Always check with your accountant how this might affect your taxable income overall. In fact, it's very wise to check with your accountant whether you need to declare your re-invested dividends as income as well.

Conclusion

Never believe that you don't have enough money to begin investing. The whole key to successful investing is starting with whatever you have. Once you've begun, work out a way to regularly add even small amounts to your existing portfolio. This might mean investing as little as $25 a week just to get you into a positive investing schedule. It might also mean re-arranging your budget and your income to work out a way to afford to put aside more money.

Regardless of your options, the sooner you get started the sooner you'll be able to begin compounding your initial efforts to start building up your stock portfolio. As your dividend earnings are re-invested back into adding more stocks to your portfolio, your overall value increases. At the same time, the amount of dividends you earn will also increase.

As long as you stick to a simple strategy, you should see very positive results. The longer you hold to your strategy and monitor your portfolio, the better your overall dividend income will be.

What's more, you're not just earning a good income from your dividends. You're also working on a solid wealth creation strategy, as your overall portfolio still has its own value. While you might think a few extra thousand dollars a year in dividend growth sounds like fun, owning a stock portfolio worth tens of thousands, or even hundreds of thousands of dollars can certainly put you closer to your goal of becoming a dividend millionaire.

Spend some time researching good quality, solid stocks that return good dividend yields. Then work on a way to get started sooner rather than later.

Passionate about Stock Investing: The Quick Guide to Investing in the Stock Market

Introduction

Have you ever thought to yourself, "If I only knew how to invest in the stock market, I'd do it?" Have you ever wondered what it would be like to be a savvy investor, sitting in the comfort of your own home as you make money with the click of a mouse? Have you been too afraid to make your dreams come true? If you answered yes to these questions, then you are like the millions of people across the globe who shares the same hang-ups, fears, and trepidations about investing in the stock market. The common thread through each of these potential investors lies in one simple word: misunderstanding.

What is keeping you from investing in the stock market, and keeping you from earning more money than you could ever dream of, is the thinking that you have to be "market minded" to be a successful investor. Conjure up your own image of an investor - they have a slick look, and can tell you at any given time how the Yen is doing in China. Your image of them is likely to be someone who's good at math and has no scruples about blowing thousands of dollars with either a "Buy" or a "Sell". This may be the investor we are used to seeing in the movies, but I'll let you in on a little secret, one that Wall Street doesn't want you to know - more and more, successful investors are regular folks, just like you, who never took a business class in their life and don't know the difference between a high rise and a low rise yet who have obtained an invaluable understanding of the market.

There is no secret code to the stock market. Rather, if you understand the terms, the patterns and what it is that will make you money, you can buy, sell and trade with the best of them.

I wrote this book to help you understand the stock market and to give you ways in which you can make money. There is no magic formula or back-alley tricks to success. All you need is knowledge of how the stock market operates and how you can find your place in the bigger picture. It's this information that is going to give you long lasting success. That's right, *long lasting*. If you're looking for quick money, you're not tapping into the full potential I'm offering in these pages. I want you to learn how to make money *for life* and I think you want the same thing too.

Before we begin, I want to lay out one ground rule. While this book is going to show you how to make money in the stock market, my larger goal is to help you achieve your financial dreams. We all want security in the knowledge that on a rainy day, there will always be something to fall back on. We all want to own a comfortable home and be able to send our children to higher education. We all want to retire when we'd planned and be able to live out our later years in comfort and style. The stock market is a means to these ends. Investing in the market is an investment in your future. You are making your money work for you. Indeed you are the key to achieving your own financial success. This is something that any financial adviser will always tell you. Making your money work for you maximizes your earning potential.

I am going to show you how to make your money work, and I want you to keep that idea running through your mind throughout the entire investing process. My one and only rule is that you remember whom you are making this money for.

Oh, and of course, have fun. You'll never do anything so exhilarating and so rewarding as making money in the stock market. If you are ready, let's begin.

Stock Market Investing

The most important thing you'll ever learn about the stock market is the language of stocks. Investors have created their own vocabulary to describe some very basic things, yet they do this to sound like they have some expert knowledge that the rest of us can't possibly begin to comprehend. They think terms like "equity" will throw non-investors off the trail of a good stock. In short, they hope that the language they've crafted will scare the masses away. Learning what the terms of the stock market are will help you learn how the stock market works.

Let's start from the very beginning; what is **investing**? Investing is the act of committing money or capital to an endeavour with the expectation of obtaining an additional income or profit. Basically, you put your money into a company so that they can use it to earn more money. You, as the investor, are taking the risks that this company is actually going to make money in the future. As a result of this risk, you are entitled to a share of the profits if and when a corporation makes them.

How do you come to own part of a company through investing? That's where **stocks** come into play. A stock is an ownership share in a corporation. When you buy a stock, you are buying a piece of a company with your investment. This is also known as **equity** or an ownership interest in a corporation.

You might hear investors say, "I just bought a 20% equity of this business for $40,000." That means they essentially own 20% of that business. It's this ownership that makes stocks so valuable. You, whoever and wherever you are, get to own part of a successful company. When it makes money, you make money. On the flip side, when it loses money, you lose money, which is an inherent risk in investing. I'll be going over risks and rewards in a later section, but for now it's important to understand that you'll reap huge benefits if the company you own stock in is successful.

There are several different kinds of stocks. First, there is **common stock**. These are also known as ordinary shares. They grant the shareholder a proportion of the company's **dividends** (payments made by a corporation to shareholders). Unfortunately, in the case of a **liquidation** (the process by which a company is brought to an end) or **bankruptcy** (when a person or organization cannot repay debts owned to creditors) of a company, common stock shareholders are one of the last creditors to be paid.

Common stock is often classified as either Class A or Class B stock and all owners of common stock have the responsibility to vote for the board of directors, Chief Financial Officer, and the Chief Executive Officer of a corporation they own stock in.

Next, we have **preferred stock**. This is a special stock sold to particular institutions or individuals that grant the holder priority over common stock holders in terms of dividends and bankruptcy claims. The dividends for a preferred stock cannot change no matter how a company is performing. Preferred stock holders are also paid first if a company fails. Preferred stocks are convertible into common stock. The draw back for preferred stock holders is that they usually don't have voting rights. The price of preferred stock will usually differ from the price of common stock, a reflection of its different rights and privileges.

Preferred stock can either be **cumulative** or **noncumulative**. A cumulative preferred stock requires that if a company fails to pay any dividend or any amount below the stated rate, it must make up for it at a later time. Dividends accumulate with each passed dividend period, which can be quarterly, semi-annually or annually. When a dividend is not paid in time, it has "passed" and all passed dividends become a debt owed to the investor, known as **arrears**. In non-cumulative preferred stocks, companies are not obliged to pay dividends at a later date if none has been declared by their board of directors in a given year.

There are actually many different kinds of preferred stock, but for now we'll stick to the basic definitions. If you decide to buy preferred stock in a company, be sure that you have outlined what the responsibilities of the company are to you and what rights you have as an investor before finalizing the purchase.

Lastly, there is **unlisted stock**. These stocks are not listed on any stock exchange and can be common or preferred. They are purchased in **non-listed securities**, also known as direct placements, from the issuer of the stocks or in the secondary market. The nature of the trading market in non-listed securities can't be predicted. While there is greater risk associated with trading "off market," these securities tend to carry higher yields than would be typically available for publicly offered securities. On the other hand, non-publicly traded securities are sometimes subject to restrictions on resale and the market for their resale is less liquid than for publicly traded securities. There is no active market in non-listed securities.

Debt securities are things like banknotes and bonds. Derivative contracts, such as futures, options, and forwards, are contracts that specify the condition of future payments.

Now, if you want to hold onto your stock in a company, that's perfectly fine. As long as that corporation keeps making money, you'll keep making money as your stock increases in value. However, if you'd like to buy and sell your stocks, you'll be **trading** them. You've probably heard on the nightly news, for example that, "IykeIsioma stock were trading at $175 today," which means that if you wanted to buy a share in the IykeIsioma Company, you'd have paid $175 for each one. Yes, I just made this up, so let's give it the stock ticker code of **IYKE**.

Many people who are interested in making money in the stock market hire a stock broker to do their trading for them. This is a very old school approach to investing. However, you really don't need a middle man involved in your investing to make money in the stock market. Everything this person is able to do, you can do with the click of a mouse or a quick phone call. Plus, you have to pay a broker to work for you. Why hire someone to do a job you can easily do yourself? In fact, as good as many brokers are, too many investors don't gain the knowledge they need to be successful independently. Let's say something happened to your stock broker and they couldn't work for you anymore. There goes all the knowledge of your stocks. You didn't develop the knowledge of the market or your individual stocks because you outsourced the job and you are left exactly where you started. You are left virtually helpless. Use a broker only if you need to, but you are perfectly capable of investing on your own and are much better off for it.

There is one investment term that will prove helpful to your understanding of the stock market yet that I won't be spending too much time on in this book. **Bonds** are a form of debt. They are like bank loans or government IOUs. You are loaning money to a corporation with the promise that they will pay you back in full with regular interest payments. Should a corporation go bankrupt, you are going to be the first person they need to pay back. Many investors view bonds as a secure investment because you are virtually guaranteed repayment plus interest. These are deemed virtually risk-free bonds. As such, these bonds, issued by the Treasury, will pay a lower yield than a bond issued by a company like General Electric (although GE is a great company to invest in, for your information, as I will be explaining in a minute).

One of my personal favourite stock market terms is "**blue chip**." This is a term used to describe stocks in corporations with a history of strong earnings, traditionally increasing dividends and an outstanding balance sheet. Companies like Pepsi, Coca-Cola, General Electric and Wal-Mart are examples of blue chip stocks. With the technology boom, many people felt that technology companies like Google, Facebook, Yahoo and eBay would completely overthrow these traditional money makers. While Google stockholders are indeed enjoying big dividends, traditional blue chip companies have not lost any earning power. In fact, many, like Wal-Mart, have increased their earnings while Internet start-ups imploded and disappeared. You might be attracted to investing in technology start-ups because technology has taken such a strong hold in the world but be wary that most of these companies do have a high rate of failure. While investors in flavour-of-the-week technology firms lose money, investors in blue chip companies are laughing all the way to the bank.

From Novice to Expert

I have by no means provided an exhaustive list of stock market terms. However, I really don't need to. I have given you what you need to begin to understand how the stock market works. In fact, these are the very terms that investors use in their day-to-day lives that they think the rest of us can't grasp. As you begin to navigate the stock market waters, you'll easily pick up any new term that comes your way. The key to success is getting your foot in the door and setting off on the right path. If you walk into the stock market blind, you'll stumble about, losing more and more of your hard earned money before finally retreating in defeat.

However, if you come in with an understanding of the terms I've laid out before you, you're already way ahead of the game.

One of the keys to long-term success in the stock market is to be a sponge. Immerse yourself in the language and the culture of stocks and corporations. If you stand on the sidelines, you'll only earn sideline money. But if you jump in feet first and push yourself to understand the stock market, you'll be extraordinarily successful. This is the key to becoming an expert in the market. World-class investors like Warren Buffett didn't let anyone but himself do his investing. He was able to achieve this by soaking up everything he could about the stock market. Learning as you go and learning from your mistakes, will help you gain an expert knowledge of the stock market.

Investing for the Future

As I mentioned in the introduction to this book, my personal take on investing is that it is an investment for my future. I am taking a certain amount of my money and putting it to work for me. I might not see the returns right away, but I know that they are coming. I can sleep soundly at night knowing that even while I rest, that money is growing. I can access it at any time or let it grow in value until I decide to use it for something like my retirement.

I am not just investing in corporations that I think are good and have a high earning power. I am investing in my future.

Optimism is the most important attitude to have in investing. You really are banking on the fact that the corporation you are putting money into is going to make money in the future. You aren't going to get your money back instantly (if you do, fantastic), but rather, over a period of time, your stocks will increase in value. You must have faith that the corporation you chose to give your money to is going to get you your money back, and then some. Don't let your optimism blind you, however. You must make wise decisions on which stocks to invest in and place your money in corporations that don't just tug at your heart but that also make sense to your head.

This is why I've also talked about long-term investing success. Pensions across the globe are diminishing. Retiring at 65 is no longer attainable for many. Investing isn't so much a way to earn some extra spending cash as it is a means to securing your future. Many are now turning to investing as a way to buy a house, pay for their children's college education, cover unexpected expenses, and to secure retirement. The reason so many people can now reap the rewards of investing is that the stock market has become infinitely more accessible in the last 15 years.

Beginners Basic Guide
to Stock Market Investment Boxed Set

Prior to the Internet, you had to hire a broker to invest your money for you or you had to be a broker yourself. Now, we can access the stock market through our laptops, iPads, and smart phones. We can day trade as we wait in line to buy coffee. The stock market has become more accessible and that means there is no reason why you can't make extra money in the comfort of your own home.

One key to success is to stay on top of the news and trends. Investing experts will tell you that an unwatched stock is an unprofitable stock. You've got to keep an eye on your money, see how it's moving, and look at the bigger picture. I've never met a successful investor that didn't know what was going on in the market. You don't have to become a stock jockey, but rather keeping abreast of the latest financial news, knowing which companies are growing, which are declining and seeing how your investments fit into the larger picture will help you make profits now and later on.

Investing is a way to build your wealth considerably. You'll remember earlier I mentioned expanding your earning potential? You can only work so many hours and earn so much as an employee. However, there is no limit to how much money you can make on the stock market except the limits you set for yourself. You can build your wealth and secure the future you've always dreamed of through smart and well-monitored investments.

Making Money in the Stock Market

There are actually quite a few ways to make money in the stock market. Unfortunately, many people never grasp how money is actually earned through stocks. I don't fault these people for not knowing because it's not something that's talked about very much. We can see how someone makes money through salary or wages, but it is very foreign to us to see how someone makes money by essentially spending their money. It's this element of trading that keeps many people away from the stock market.

One of the most sure fire ways to build your wealth and invest in your future is if you start investing *right now* and taking advantage of **compounding interest.** Your investments need time to mature. The difference of ten years is huge in terms of investing. Consider this scenario. Two people, both age 25. One of them, we'll call her Nneka, invests $15,000 at an interest rate of 5.5%. Let's assume that the interest rate compounds annually (I'll be speaking about compounding interest in just a little bit). By the time Nneka is 50, she will have $57,200.89 ($15,000 x 1.055 for 25 years) in her bank account.

The other 25-year-old, we'll call him Ade, waits until he's 35. He invests the same amount as Nneka, $15,000, at the same interest rate of 5.5% compounded annually. By the time Ade is 50, he'll only have $33,487.15($15,000 x 1.055 for 15 years) in his bank account.

Nneka has $23,713.74 more in her bank account than Ade, even though he invested the same amount of money. However, Nneka gave her investment time to grow and ended up earning a total of $42,200.89 in interest and Ade only earned $18,487.15.

The earlier you start investing, the more time your money has to accrue interest and earn you more money. An investment that is made early earns interest and, before long, that interest starts to earn interest. By the time Nneka is 60, she'll have close to $100,000 in her account, whereas Ade would only have close to $60,000.

This is the principle of compounding interest. Not every kind of investment will give you this kind of interest growth, but it is one of the avenues you can take.

Another way to make money in the stock market is through **capital appreciation**.

Capital appreciation refers to the rise in price of your shares, allowing you to make a profit if or when you sell them. Remember, that as an investor you are in it for the long haul, your goal being to preserve your capital as well as to increase it.

People who bought stock in blue chip companies early for a low price have been able to turn around and sell them for far more than they paid, earning return rates of many hundreds of dollars per stock.

The second way you can make money in the stock market is through the payment of dividends. You'll remember earlier in this book I defined dividends as payments made to stockholders.

Many companies will pay their investors every six months or once a year. What they are essentially trying to do by paying investors is to give them their investment back and show them that the company is making money and therefore is worth continued investment. What many companies do now is wait a number of years as their value rises and hold off paying investors. They'll then make a large payment to investors once the corporation reaches a desirable valuation.

Whether you own common stock or preferred stock, getting paid dividends is a sure fire way to make money on the stock market, as long as the corporation you've invested in is making money. Some companies experience a few bad quarters every once in a while, so if you can ride out the bad times and wait for the corporation to pick its earnings back up, you might just be rewarded with a fantastic dividend payment.

The Tools of the Trade

All you really need in this day and age to make money in the stock market is a computer with a good Internet connection. If you have access to all your stocks, financial news, prices, updates, and press releases, you are leaps and bounds ahead of the game. Once you've got your computer hooked up, I recommend utilizing an online trading system. There are many of these on the market.

Some will offer you updates on prices while others will give you trade recommendations.

Where you get your information on stocks and the market will be a vital part of your success in trading. Having up-to-date and accurate information could mean success or failure. I suggest joining an online trading forum to exchange ideas and get tips on where to invest, what to buy and when to sell. The reason I say this is because much of your work regarding stock market will be carried out online. Forums, just so you know, are online communities of people who share a common interest. There are golfing forums, baking forums and trading forums. While you've got to be cautious that the forum you belong to is reputable and the people on them aren't just trying to rip you off, when you find a good forum, the information gained there is worth as much as your stock holdings.

Many forums cater for certain stock niches, such as technology, crude commodities or the American market. If you are finding that you prefer one kind of stock over the other, then these types of forums can be invaluable to you as you gain a deeper understanding of that particular market. Of course,

Beginners Basic Guide
to Stock Market Investment Boxed Set

you can enter into any forum on any subject, so don't feel limited. If you've always been interested in investing in silver, for example, find a forum that caters for people who deal in precious metals and learn more about that market before committing your money to some stocks.

Some great forums to check out when you are first starting out are: www.SiliconInvestor.com, www.Swing-Trade-Stocks.com and www.theLion.com. Naturally, you may not like these forums and find some on your own that you prefer. It's really up to you where you choose to get your knowledge and who you interact with.

Lastly, read the newspapers and other financial sources. Like I mentioned earlier, staying on top of the trends and latest market news is tantamount to success. You don't want to find out two weeks later that there was a strike at the mine you invested in and as a result lost thousands because product couldn't be extracted. It pays, in more ways than one, to know what is going on in the world. As time goes on, you'll be able to spot trends and anticipate the market based on larger socio-economic factors, which any investor will tell you is the real way to make money. Green technology, for example, is a slow yet steadily growing market that is going to make those who've invested in it very wealthy later down the road.

Myths

Before you picked up this book, and probably even as you're reading it, you held some pretty firm beliefs about the stock market. While you probably think of it as a way to make a lot of money, you also likely hold a lot of hang-ups and anxieties about putting the cash you have in hand into something that seems so volatile.

I want to address some fears and myths that many people hold about investing before we go any further so you can commit to this endeavour and feel sure that your money is going to be as safe and secure as possible.

One of the biggest misconceptions about investing is that it is akin to gambling. The belief is that you're basically placing thousands of dollars on the table, rolling the dice, and hoping to land on lucky seven. This couldn't be further from the truth in terms. Yes, investing can be like gambling if you don't know what you are doing. In gambling, you have absolutely no control over the circumstances surrounding your money. The ball is either going to land on black or red and there's nothing you can do about it. Investing allows you much more control. It also requires that you maintain as much control over your money as possible to be successful. Investing that is likened to gambling will be for example, when you close your eyes, pick a stock out of the paper and throw your money at it. Investing involves research and analysis in order for it to be effective. It takes prior knowledge to decide whether there is a reasonable expectation of profit in any given investment. While you can't control the stock market, you can always sell your stocks or buy more or totally pull out whenever you choose. In gambling, once your chips are down, that's it.

You might hear from traders in forums and financial advisors elsewhere that avoiding aggressive investments is the best way to minimize losses in a market downturn and keep your money safe. You might even think like this yourself, especially if you have a more cautious personality. However, non-aggressive investments have their own set of hidden downsides.

One factor that many first-time investors ignore is inflation. Even though you might keep your principle whole, if you earn less than the inflation rate, your money losses its purchasing power. Taxes also play into this situation and adversely affect the value of your money.

Many aggressive investments will preserve the purchasing power of your money and add to your principal over time. Combined with a smart investing strategy and diverse investments, the risk will be minimized and hopefully boosts returns. Lastly, many people don't go into investing because they think they need an MBA or at least a business background and a good understanding of economics to be good at it. This, as I hope you can see in this book, is far from the truth. All you really need to be successful in the stock market is some financial basics, all of which I've tried to lay out for you as this book has progressed.

Risks

Now, I don't want you to think that just because I told you that investing isn't the same as gambling, there are no risks involved. As with any business, there is inherent risk in putting your money towards future earnings. Why? It is because those earnings aren't in the bank yet. You are taking a chance that what you are investing in is going to make money down the road and putting your faith, and your money, into that hope.

There are a few risks that every investor faces. One of the most obvious risks of investing is that the economy can experience a downturn. We saw this happen in 1929 and we saw it happen again in 2001 and 2008. The economy is affected by a number of factors; war, civil unrest, a natural disaster, etc. There is nothing you and I can do to control these elements and therefore nothing we can do to turn the economy around on our own. The best strategy to dealing with a bad economy is to be determined and ride it out. With every dip in the economy comes an upswing. We've seen it happen many times and it will continue going up and down long after we've traded in the market. When the economy is bad, do what you can to increase your position in blue chip companies that can weather economic storms. This way you can still earn while not incurring too many risks. Older investors might find that because they are close to retirement, a major downturn in stocks can be devastating. The best thing for someone in that situation is to anticipate a downturn as much as possible (read the newspapers) and shift a significant number of assets to more secure bonds or fixed income securities.

Inflation is another risk that investors have to look out for. Inflation affects everyone, not just investors, and destroys values while creating recessions. Inflation hurts investors on fixed incomes the most because it affects the value of their income stream. When inflation is high, investors have historically turned to "hard assets" such as real estate and precious metals, especially gold.

Lastly, it is vital to take certain risks in order to achieve your financial goals rather than just being a conservative investor.

One of the thrills of the market is finding that stock that makes you more money than you ever dreamed possible. Don't shy away from opportunities that your gut is telling you to take. They could be well worth it.

The best way to minimize your risks is to be prepared. Just like you wouldn't go rock climbing without ropes and a plan on how you are going to scale the mountain, you can't go into investing unequipped with the proper tools and knowledge. Unless you want to lose your money, which I doubt you do, you've got to do the research and analysis to make sure that a very sound decision is made. Of course, even after the most careful research, you still might lose money, but that's ok. It doesn't have to spell the end for your time as an investor. The most valuable commodity you have is knowledge, so if you can walk away from a loss having gained experience and learned what to do differently next time, you've actually earned something quite invaluable. It's only if you keep making the same mistakes over and over that it might be time to consider getting out of the trading business.

Rewards

Now, the most coveted reward of investing in the stock market is the most obvious one: to make money.

The stock market might just be one of the most interesting, exhilarating, and sure way to make money, if done properly. America, and the world, are full of people who made millions by learning how the stock market works, taking risks when it was right and diversifying their stocks. These people had the conviction to ride out sour economic times and did their homework on how, where, and when to invest. It takes time and a few stumbles, but you can achieve that same level of financial success as well.

An added benefit of trading in the stock market is the knowledge you gain about companies. You are literally there for every rise and fall in their value, every product launch, every board change and you get to see virtually firsthand how they operate. You might even pick up enough knowledge to open your own business based on what you observe in the corporations that you have invested in. With that, you also get to see how the economy functions. Watching the stock market is like watching a part - a very important part of the overall economy. Many financial experts will advise their clients to keep an eye on the macroeconomic factors that affect the market, things like war, inflation, employment rates, etc. By working in the stock market, you can learn how the economy reacts to different macroeconomic factors and learn to spot and anticipate trends before they happen. This will help you be a better investor.

You've probably heard the old adage, "The greater the risk, the greater the reward?" This phrase is completely applicable to the stock market for several reasons. If you invest conservatively and feel more comfortable keeping the majority of your assets in high interest savings accounts, that's perfectly fine. However, if you are willing to put a higher percentage of your income and/or savings into more aggressive investments and those investments are successful, you'll get higher returns.

Secondly, if you put your money into riskier investments, you also stand to earn a lot more than if you stick with safe investments. This is because safe investments will earn you money over time and that's a good thing. However, it's not going to be the same kind of money you'd see if you invest in a business with a high potential for quick growth.

The risk of course with the quick-growth company is that it may stagnate and drop in value, taking the value of your stocks with it. If that happens you're left with a choice; take the hit and sell your stocks for less than you paid for or hang onto them and wait to see if the price picks up again. When the price is high, you can sell the stocks, getting a higher return on your investment. Herein lies the risk of investing. You never know how things are going to play out. What makes you rich one day might make you a pauper the next. It really takes time to get a read on the pulse of the stock market, plus a hefty amount of intuition, to know when to hang onto your stocks and when to sell. Take comfort in the fact that for every great investment Warren Buffett has made, he's made his share of gaffes. No investor is 100 percent right all of the time and you won't be either. The key is to keep preserving, learn from your mistakes, and know when to reap your rewards.

Be a Wise Investor

Unlike gambling, it is possible to be wise with your money in the stock market. You aren't just throwing it blindly to the wind and hoping it sticks somewhere. You can be smart, and there are few factors to consider before you decide how to invest your money.

Don't invest in something that you aren't interested in. To paraphrase Mark Cuban, self-made billionaire and owner of the Dallas

Mavericks, don't get involved in something that you just don't have a personal attraction to. You've got to fall in love with your investments if you hope to really make them work well for you. If you invest in something you don't really know about and have no interest in, you'll get bored and even resentful of the corporation that has your money, especially if it's doing poorly. It helps to believe in the corporation you've invested into, so that way you can weather the storms and ride the highs with them.

Age, income level and long-term goals all play into what you invest in. They don't have to be determining factors; just because you are 55 doesn't mean you can't invest in new companies. Just be smart about what you commit to. You want to have the energy and the enthusiasm to get involved with your stocks. If you don't have the revenue, energy, or conviction to stick with a stock, then you are better off without it.

Strategies That Work

Every stockholder is different and each has their own strategies of how to work the stock market. There is no foolproof strategy when it comes to picking stocks. This simply does not exist. What you can do is analyze a company's fundamentals. What is its value, based on future profit potential? What were the company's earnings in the past and how do they stack up the future projections? By answering these questions, you can decide if a company is going to earn you money and get you a return on your investment.

Personally, I like to look at my ownership of stocks as actual ownership in the underlying business. This helps me think about the fundamentals of the business such as profitability, cash flows, management capabilities and the industry trends. I can then research the business in depth; focus on what is really driving the company and whether that is going to lead to sustained growth. This strategy has helped me stick with stocks that had some rough patches yet took a huge upswing with high profits. You will become successful if you look at the business as a whole and not just the stocks and the market.

You've got to scrutinize the businesses you invest into, to truly know if they are the right places for your money. What excites you about a business? What are the issues that you need the company to focus on? Are they focusing on resolving these issues? Is the company generating income and cash flow that you think the business is capable of? Is the company the best in the industry in turning a profit and providing a superior product or service?

Understanding the businesses you invest in is one of the best strategies you can take. If you can't read financial statements in detail and understand each and every line item, you shouldn't be investing in the business. There are too many things you'll miss if you can't come to know the business.

Additionally, it is vital that you understand the team that is running the business. The people at the helm of the corporation you are investing in will have a direct impact on your money. Make sure they deserve all the money you give them.

Perfecting Your Portfolios

A portfolio is a combination of different investment assets mixed and matched for the purpose of achieving an investor's goals. Items that are considered as part of your portfolio can include any asset you own - from real items such as art and real estate, to equities, fixed-income instruments and their cash and equivalents. For the purpose of this section, we will focus on the most liquid asset types: equities, fixed-income securities, cash and equivalents.

An easy way to think of a portfolio is to imagine a pie chart, whose portions each represent a type of vehicle to which you have allocated a certain portion of your whole investment. The asset mix you choose according to your aims and strategy will determine the risk and expected return of your portfolio.

There are few different types of basic portfolios. Aggressive investment strategies - those that shoot for the highest possible return - are most appropriate for investors who, for the sake of this potential high return, have a high-risk tolerance. Generally, aggressive portfolios have a higher investment in equities. A moderately aggressive portfolio would consist of approximately 50-55% equities, 35-40% bonds, and 5-10% cash and cash equivalents. Of course, you can further break down each class into subclasses, such as the equities into large and small companies, the bonds into short and long-term, government versus corporate etc.

Conservative investment strategies put security at a high priority. Conservative portfolios will generally consist mainly of cash and cash equivalents or high-quality fixed-income instruments. The main goal of a conservative portfolio strategy is to maintain the real value of the portfolio or to protect the value of the portfolio against inflation. It might consist of bonds and high quality equities, which would yield long-term capital growth potential.

There are two types of portfolio management; passive and active. Passive investors rely on the stock market's history of increasing over the long-term and will purchase a security such as an index fund, which is a type of mutual fund in a portfolio constructed to match or track the components of a market index, such as Standard & Poor's 500 Index (the S&P 500). An index mutual fund provides broad market exposure, low operating expenses and a low portfolio turnover. The strategy behind active portfolio investment is to select securities that will perform better than the overall market. In these cases, the investor is trying to beat the market.

Diversifying

Diversification is the most important component of your investment plan. Portfolios all play into diversification.

Different securities perform differently at any time, so with a mix of asset types, your entire portfolio does not suffer the impact of a decline of any one security. Investing this way is like a balancing act. The scale never gets tipped too far one way or the other and you are able to maintain your moneymaking ability no matter if one or more of your stocks is on the decline.

The purpose of diversification is to reduce risk by holding non-correlated investments. Studies have shown that risk reduction through diversification becomes negligible once you hold about 25-30 securities across sectors and industries. If you spread your investments around, you aren't putting all your eggs into one basket, therefore reducing the risk of catastrophic financial losses.

Don't worry about diversifying when you first start out, unless you are planning to invest *a large* sum of money, because it would be unwise to put a large sum into one stock. Start small and get a feel for the stock market before you start diversifying your portfolio. You don't want to wait too long as this could affect your earning potential and put you in danger of losing all your money, but take the time to research which stocks out there are right for you and which ones are going to make your portfolio profitable.

I Can Do This at Home

Absolutely. You can do this at home. All it takes is a computer, an Internet connection, and some investment of time and energy on your part to make the best investment choices possible. It also takes keeping a close eye on your investments. If you don't keep on top of what your money is doing, then you risk losing it all. But, if you keep on top of trends and projections, you are in a much better position to make a lot of money in the stock market.

Using an online trading service like E*Trade or TD Ameritrade will aid in your efforts to invest online at home. It pays to have as many tools at your disposal when investing, so investing in software or services that help you invest wisely is a smart move. You can be as active or as passive as you like with these services. You might check your stocks once a day or once an hour. It's completely up to you how much commitment you give your stocks, which is another benefit of trading from home. You can still live a normal life and make money through your investments. Remember, your money is working for you even while you're off the clock.

You might come to a point in your investing where you feel lost, confused or like you aren't maximizing your investments. If that's the case, then it might be prudent to meet with a financial adviser to get another perspective on your strategy. They might have some insight into how you can invest more wisely.

However, be warned that they, like business people, are looking for new clients, so they will likely try to sign you up for their services. If this is something you feel would be the right choice for you, then don't hesitate to hire a professional. As I've mentioned time and time again, you have all the tools you need to start investing and to start making money in the stock market. All you need is some fundamental knowledge (which I've set out to give you in this book), and confidence in yourself to make it happen.

Success Stories

I have seen just about every type of person in every walk of life succeed in the stock market which goes to show that everyone has access to the market via their computers.

The stock market does have its pitfalls, especially for those that go in unprepared. However, it is not the scary, foreign terrain that you probably have always thought it was. It is an exciting, interesting and lucrative business that can help you secure the financial future you've always wanted. The best part is you can do this all at home. By studying the market and immersing yourself in the businesses you invest in, you can achieve real success in the stock market.

Warning: Prior to choosing where to invest your money, it is very important that you do some research.
Your capital is at risk when you invest in stocks - you can lose some or all of your money, so never risk more than you can afford to lose. Always seek professional advice if you are unsure about the

Beginners Basic Guide to Stock Market Investment Boxed Set

suitability of any investment. Past performance is not a reliable indicator of future results.

Check Out Other Books:

Investing in Gold and Silver Bullion - The Ultimate Safe Haven Investments

Nigerian Stock Market Investment: 2 Books with Bonus Content

Economic Crisis: Surviving Global Currency Collapse - Safeguard Your Financial Future with Silver and Gold

Guide to Investing in the Nigerian Stock Market

**Beginners Basic Guide
to Stock Market Investment Boxed Set**

Building Wealth with Dividend Stocks in the Nigerian Stock Market (Dividends - Stocks Secret Weapon)

The Beginners Basic Guide to Investing in Gold and Silver Boxed Set

Precious Metals Investing For Beginners: The Quick Guide to Platinum and Palladium

Bitcoin and Digital Currency for Beginners: The Basic Little Guide

Child Millionaire: Stock Market Investing for Beginners - How to Build Wealth the Smart Way for Your Child - The Basic Little Guide.

If you would like to share this book with another person, please purchase an additional copy for each recipient. Thank you for respecting the hard work of this author.

www.ingramcontent.com/pod-product-compliance
Lightning Source LLC
Chambersburg PA
CBHW071756170526
45167CB00003B/1054